Today my friend Jerry is coming over to play.

We like to run and play outside, but today it is raining.

What shall we play?

Toy box

"Let's play dressing up," I say.

"I will be a beautiful princess."

"OK," says Jerry.

"I want to be a knight."

Dressing-up clothes

4

Mum's old dress is too big for me. But I feel like a princess.

Mum finds Jerry a helmet. "You might meet a dragon!" she says.

Dressing up

"What shall we play?" asks Jerry.

"Let's build a castle," I say.

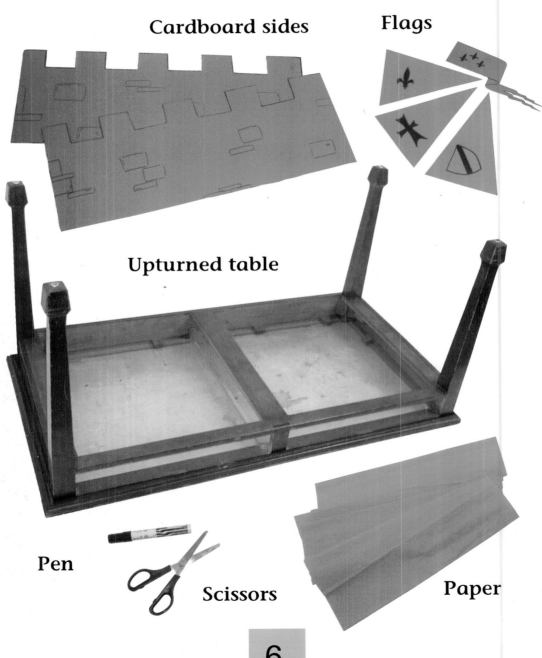

Cardboard sides

Flags

Upturned table

Pen

Scissors

Paper

Mum helps us to build the castle.

"Now we are safe from dragons," says Jerry.

Castle

We leave our castle and have a peek outside. The sun is out!

"Come on, let's jump on the trampoline," says Jerry.

On the trampoline

Then we play hopscotch.
I throw a stone. I hop, hop, hop
all the way to the end.

I stand on one leg and
pick up the stone.

Hopscotch

"Your brother is playing football. Do you want to watch?" Dad asks.

"Can we play, too?" I ask. "You can play after the match," says Dad.

Football match

At the match, I cheer for Will's team. "Go on, Will!" I shout.

The players take a rest at half-time. Jerry and I play catch with the ball.

Playing catch

After the match, Will plays with us.

He kicks the ball to me.

Then I kick the ball to Jerry.

"Shoot!" says Will. Jerry kicks the ball hard. It goes into the net!

"It's a goal!" I shout.

Scoring a goal

In the car

Dad drives us home in the car.

"What shall we play?" I ask.

"Let's play I Spy," says Dad.
"Will, you go first."

"I spy with my little eye, something beginning with W," says Will.

We all look out the car window. What begins with a W?

Looking out of the car

"Tree," says Dad.

We all laugh.
"Tree doesn't
begin with a W,"
says Will.

Tree

Window

"Window,"
says Jerry.

"Yes,"
says Will.
"You got it!"

"Now it's Jerry's turn to ask,"
says Dad.

"I spy something that begins with B,"
says Jerry. Can you see what it is?

At home, Mum is cooking dinner.
"What shall we play now?" I ask.

"How about a game of
draughts?" says Dad.

**Playing
draughts**

I move the black pieces and Jerry moves the white.

Can you see where I can jump over Jerry's piece?

Draughts board

It is time for dinner,
and Jerry goes home.

After dinner, we play Snap.
Mum helps me sort my cards.

Playing cards

After we finish, I start to yawn.

"It's time for a sleepy girl and her teddy to go to bed," says Dad. "You can play again tomorrow!"

Teddy

Here are some words and
phrases from the book.

Dressing up

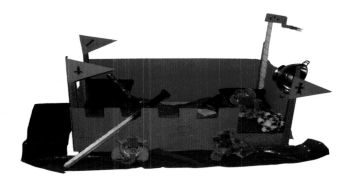

Castle

Play cards

Look in the toy box

Jump on the trampoline

Hopscotch

Play draughts

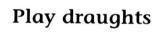

Kick the ball

Can you use these words to write your own story?

Did you see these in the book?

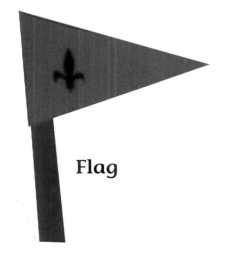

Flag

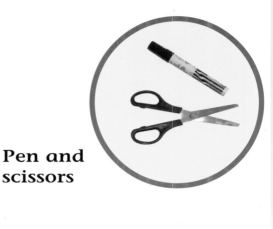

Pen and
scissors

Hat

Board game

© Aladdin Books Ltd 2001
All rights reserved
Designed and produced by
Aladdin Books Ltd
28 Percy Street
London W1T 2BZ
Literacy Consultant
Rosemary Chamberlin
Printed in U.A.E.

First published in
Great Britain in 2001 by
Franklin Watts
96 Leonard Street
London EC2A 4XD

A catalogue record for this
book is available from the
British Library.

ISBN 0 7496 4845 7

Illustrator
Mary Lonsdale - SGA

Picture Credits
All photos by Select
Pictures except 8, 23tl
– Corbis.